NEW APPROACH TOWARDS AFRICA'S DEVELOPMENT

LESSONS FROM SINGAPORE

KOFI & AKUA GYAN

NEW APPROACH TOWARDS AFRICA'S DEVELOPMENT
© Copyright, 2019 by KOFI & AKUA GYAN

ISBN: **9789-9885-40692**
Published by:
Initiators Multimedia
(The book publishing division of Initiators Group, LLC)
P. O .Box KD 841, Kanda
Accra-Ghana
Initiators2014@gmail.com

+233 (0)243571237
+233 (0)262571237

For your personal copy of this book, information about other books by the publisher, bulk purchase, please contact +233 (0)505719369

Designed in Accra, Ghana by: Initiators Multimedia

NEW APPROACH TOWARDS AFRICA'S DEVELOPMENT

LESSONS FROM SINGAPORE

KOFI & AKUA GYAN

FOREWORD

Since the 1950s various scholars have attempted to explain the problem of underdevelopment in the Third World by propounding several development theories.

Essentially, these theories are about how desirable positive change in society can best be achieved. The tendency was to oversimplify, and homogenize complex identities and diversities in the political and social systems of the Third World.

As a result, developing countries have tended to adopt strategies that are rather foreign and difficult to reconcile with local circumstances. Critics have argued that these theories, in reality, either offer little solution to or exacerbate the developmental problems of the Third World. In fact, developing countries end up being client states rather than succeed in finding indigenous solutions to their problems. This is because, over time, industrialized powers have found ways to either frustrate such strategies or cause them to work to their own advantage.

Without doubt sub-Saharan Africa, for instance, has received a fair dosage of developmental strategies and yet serious challenges to development still remain. In spite of these limitations, some countries have managed to fashion out development strategies that have enabled them move from Third World status to become what is known today as Newly Industrialized Countries.

This book focuses on Singapore as a model of Newly Industrialized Countries. It is full of material and insights and it considers a wide range of developmental issues. These are examined in the light of key development theories and scholarship. Its main argument is that development in underdeveloped economies has suffered from a lack of indigenous, contextual and relevant development model.

A central thesis of this book is therefore based on the need to understand the dynamic interplay between development theories and practice and offers an alternate viewpoint based on a deeper understanding of local contexts.

The book does not only makes serious intellectual contribution to the development discourse but it also provides invaluable pointers to new thinking, policies and actions that the developing world must engage in to come out of its dependency model onto a pathway of growth, development and prosperity. This book, therefore, stands the chance of being a reference point for many years.

PROFESSOR ATO ESSUMAN
DEAN OF FACULTY OF EDUCATION & ENTREPRENEURSHIP
METHODIST UNIVERSITY COLLEGE GHANA
FORMER MEMBER OF THE COUNCIL OF STATE
FORMER CHIEF DIRECTOR OF MINISTRY OF EDUCATION

DEDICATION

To all Africans who have a burning desire to be Initiators of Change.

ACKNOWLEDGEMENT

We are forever grateful to the Almighty God for the gift of life and the abundant blessings He has bestowed on us throughout our lives. He may be only God to many people but for us He is also our father and our everything. Without Him we are nothing.

Before we acknowledge anybody else, let us take this opportunity to thank our parents for their many sacrifices and the invaluable investments they have made in us by which we are able to share this book with the world and become a blessing to our generation and those after.

Also, we thank our beautiful Princesses, Ama, Adwoa, and Afia. We couldn't have asked God for more. Your display of intelligence even at your tender ages gives us a lot of hope and inspiration for a better African continent and world.

We specially thank the Life Patron of Initiators of Change Foundation (ICF), His Excellency John Agyekum Kufuor, Former President of the Republic of Ghana for his belief in and support for what we do at the Foundation.

Equally, we appreciate the highly respected and dedicated Board of Trustees of ICF: Most Rev. Dr. Aboagye-Mensah, Prof. Miranda Greenstreet, Hon. Kwame Amporfo Twumasi, Prof. S.K.B.Asante, Ambassador Alex Ntim Abankwa, Dr. Joyce Aryee, Dr. Isaac Owusu Mensah, and Rev. Dr. Nana Yaa Owusu-Prempeh for their wise counsel and direction that have brought us this far.

Lastly, we thank our team at the Initiators Group, Mr. Seth Duodu, Mr. Kwaku Arthur, and Mr. Ampomah Benjamin for supporting the vision of inspiring generations for a better world.

CONTENT

INTRODUCTION

Third World states have been in search of adding self-sufficiency to political freedom since independence. However, sustainable solutions to developmental problems in developing countries remain elusive. The reason is that, these countries have often adopted strategies that have not been able to reconcile local circumstances with the ever increasing demands of the international climate. This suggests the need for a new approach to transformation and growth. The "miracle" of Singapore to achieve self-sustaining socio-economic growth by combining indigenous strategies with elements of Western paradigms, seems to indicate that there are other dimensions to the problem of underdevelopment that have not been considered.

What makes Singapore unique from other Third World countries with a similar history of colonialism and political upheavals? Can the Singapore experience offer a new approach for Third World development? This book, among others, seeks answers to these questions.

This book examines the development experience of Singapore over a forty-year period (1965 to 2005). Representation of the development experience of the Third World is limited to Africa given that out of 46 countries worldwide classified as least developed (in per capita incomes), 31 are in Africa.

To this end this book is aimed at analysing the following:

a)To examine the nature of Singapore's development.

b) To identify Singapore's strategy in surviving various developmental hurdles that have retarded growth and development in Africa.

c) To examine the possibility of a new approach to development in Africa based on lessons from Singapore.

d) To contribute to the enhancement of policy decisions of African governments in particular and attempt to propose sustainable solutions to Africa's developmental bottlenecks as well as further research into Third World development.

We live in a very dynamic and competitive world. The longer it takes to find an appropriate development strategy for the Third World, the greater the probability of battling with more challenges and increased marginalization. The fact that rigid Western development paradigms have not been entirely successful suggests that development is a multidimensional process and must not be limited to ideals from one side of the globe. This book is aimed at discussing a new approach to reaching the goal of self-sufficiency in Third World countries.

The book is based on the theory of Economic Nationalism.

The central idea of the theory is that the state must be the predominant actor in international relations and serve as an instrument of economic development. Nationalists also emphasize the primacy of national security, and of military power in the organization and functioning of the international system.

According to Robert Gilpin, Economic Nationalists are of the view that the struggle among states for economic resources is an inherent feature of the international system itself. Hence states are in a constant search for ways to benefit most from opportunities and secure a good economic standing, which in itself, is a sign of national power. Furthermore, although economic nationalism has taken several different forms in the modern world, the desire for power and independence has remained an overriding concern.

A close examination of the development process of Singapore reveals that socio-economic transformation was largely state-led. There was a strong need to survive as an independent but vulnerable state amidst pessimism from the international community. The survival of the young state hinged on strong leadership, positive nationalistic attitudes, industrialization, a desire for excellence and sound national security policies.

CHAPTER ONE

SINGAPORE'S DEVELOPMENT STRATEGY SINCE INDEPENDENCE

The ability of Singapore (a dot on the world map) to achieve sustained economic growth in a highly competitive international political economy, was thus regarded as a miracle. What Singapore's early leaders sought was to create what Lee Kuan Yew terms "a First World Oasis in a Third World Region."[1] This chapter examines the forty-year developmental trajectory of Singapore from independence to the new millennium. Taking into consideration the tendency for analysts to overemphasize the economic dimension of development, this chapter also delves into the political and social dimensions of growth. Political stability and social reform played a very important role in fostering growth in Singapore.

A BRIEF HISTORY OF SINGAPORE

The Republic of Singapore is an independent city-state in South East Asia. It comprises one major island and 59 small adjacent islets, located off the southern tip of the Malay Peninsula. The city of Singapore is at the south-eastern end of the island. It is one of the most important port cities and commercial centres of South East Asia. The total area of the republic is 685 sq km (265 sq miles). It is believed that Singapore was a trading centre in the Malay kingdom of Sri Vijaya until the 14th century, when title passed to the kingdom of Majapahit. It was claimed in the 15th century by the Malacca (Melaka) sultanate under Tun Perak.

The modern city was founded in 1819 by the British colonial administrator Sir Thomas Stamford Raffles, on the site of a fishing village. Its advantageous location on the narrow passage between the Indian Ocean and the South China Sea and its free-port status soon turned Singapore into a major commercial centre, especially after the opening of the Suez Canal in 1869. The population grew through British-supported emigration, with the Chinese becoming a majority in Singapore over Malays and Indians. In 1921, Britain designated the island its principal naval base in East Asia and undertook extensive military construction.

During World War II, Singapore was captured and occupied by Japanese forces in February 1942 in a weeklong campaign that followed their conquest of British Malaya. Anti-Japanese resistance by Singaporeans, including such notable heroes as Lim Bo Seng, was met with stern repression. On September 6, 1945, the city was liberated by British troops. The following year, Singapore was made a separate Crown Colony from Malaya.

In 1955, responsibility for domestic policy passed to the locally elected ministers and legislative assembly, and on June 3, 1959, Singapore became a self-governing state in the Commonwealth of Nations. On September 16, 1963, Singapore, Malaya, North Borneo (renamed Sabah), and Sarawak united to form Malaysia.

However, in 1965 Singapore separated from Malaysia, owing to differences with the federal government, and became a sovereign state. She remained in the Commonwealth and became a member of the United Nations (UN) in September 1965. In December of that year the island was proclaimed a republic.[2] Inche Yusof bin Ishak, head of state since 1959, became the first president. His successors were Prof. Benjamin Henry Sheares (1971-1981), Chengara Veetil Devan Nair (1981-1985), Wee Kim Wee (1985-1993) and Ong Teng Cheong (1993-1999). The current president is Halimah Yacob, who was elected unopposed at the 2017 presidential election. She is the first female President of Singapore and first Malay head of state in 47 years since the death of Yusof Ishak, Singapore's first president. Before 1993 the president was appointed by parliament for four-year terms. Currently Presidents are elected. The first Prime Minister was Lee Kuan Yew (1959-1990). His successors are

Goh Chok Tong (1990-2004) and Lee Hsien Loong (2004 to date). While the Prime Minister is the head of government, the position of President is largely ceremonial.

IMMEDIATE POST-INDEPENDENCE CHALLENGES THAT INFLUENCED DEVELOPMENT POLICIES

Independence was achieved amidst tears rather than laughter. Lee Kuan Yew describes post independent Singapore as a nation kicked out of the Malaysian Federation with no signposts to the next destination. Indeed, the general prediction of the international community was that the city-state had an improbable chance of survival. One writer of a foreign newspaper compared Britain's withdrawal from the colony to "the decline of the Roman Empire when law and order collapsed as the Romans withdrew and Barbarian Hordes took over."[3] Singapore needed to gain international recognition as an independent and viable state.

The internal socio-political climate was equally turbulent. The PAP inherited a society that was economically divided, and communally fragmented and inchoate. **Political rivalry** was rife as there was a multitude of political groupings, each representing a specific economic or ethnic identification.

At independence, Singapore appeared to be burdened with poor economic prospects. Following the expulsion, there was no sign of an opportunity to be part of a regional common market to supplement her small domestic market.

To worsen the situation was Singapore's declining entrepot trade. In fact, Malaysia had decided to bypass Singapore and trade directly with trading partners, importers and exporters. Hence, import substitution that was the economic trend of the day, was not a viable option. Other mitigating economic conditions included dependence on British military spending, low productivity and chronic unemployment (over 14%).[4] Labour relations were poor owing to endless strikes, slowdowns and riots. By the mid 1960s, Communists had gained control of most unions. Eventually, both Communists and non-Communist unions had turned combative. The government's challenge was to free unions from Communist control and detrimental labour habits learnt under British rule.

National security was another major concern of the young city-state. Singapore had depended on British military presence for security since colonial rule. At independence, the state had neither a standing army of her own nor military logistics. Singapore's hope was that the British will not pull out before the young state was strong enough to establish her own military. One implication of British decline was that Singapore would no longer have Britain to serve as a buffer against any threats from the United States (which at the time was deep in the Cold War and very unpopular over the Vietnam War, especially among Third World countries).[5]

Another possible external threat was the threat of a coup by Malay extremists in Kuala Lumpur, which could spill over to Singapore. Singapore also feared that her independent status would be reversed if there was a change of government in Malaysia.[6] Internally, majority of policemen were Malays while two Singaporean Battalions were under the command of a Malaysian Brigadier. How was loyalty to the new government and nation to be assured? In view of these threats, there was a very urgent need to build an army and to enforce the rule of law to protect Singapore's fragile independence.

Some Favourable Conditions

Aside these internal constraints, Singapore was fortunate to find herself in an emerging global economy that was favourable. The 1960s saw rapid economic growth for all industrialized countries. Singapore thus had to decide either to take advantage of the economic climate or resign herself to the uncertainty of the future ahead.

Internally, although Singapore had no natural resources, she had hardworking people, good basic infrastructure, and a government determined to be honest and competent. The government had the trust and confidence of the people.[7] The challenge was to maximize the utility of the few assets available.

How was a country about 15,000 times smaller than the USA to survive? The government's challenge was to build a nation out of a disparate collection of immigrants and make a living for the people. This was regardless of the fact that Singapore's role as the entrepot of the region was becoming defunct. Weighing the options available, the PAP government decided to make a living different from what pertained under British rule. Singapore could not afford to remain satisfied with being a processing and grading centre of raw materials for Malaysia and Indonesia. The government, taking cognisance of pessimistic signals from all sides, saw the need to muster extraordinary confidence. Lee Kuan Yew saw it as his duty to give the people hope rather than demoralize them. In the following comments he gives a clear picture of the government's strategy for survival:

"After pondering these problems and the limited options available, I concluded an Island City-State in Southeast Asia could not be ordinary if it was to survive. We had to make extraordinary efforts to become a tightly knit, rugged and adaptable people who could do things better and cheaper than our neighbours... (we needed to create) a new kind of economy...try new methods and schemes...we had to be different...because there was no other country like Singapore."[8]

POLITICAL DEVELOPMENT

To gain substantive international recognition, the government appointed Sinnathamby Rajaratnam as Foreign Minister. The criteria included the following: a person who was able, credible and possessed the right balance between standing up for principles and the need for diplomatic compromise.

According to Khong Cho-oon, to maximize economic growth Lee Kuan Yew did not strictly follow a specific political model.[9] Instead he adopted an eclectic approach whereby he applied elements of a political model as and when it suited the government's developmental objectives or specific needs of the country. Cho-oon is of the opinion that in spite of the eclectic trend, Communitarianism seems to have been Singapore's fundamental political strategy from the start.

He asserts that in Singapore's communitarian system, the aim is to build a society in which every citizen enjoys a fair share of national resources. Certain civic values are promoted to curb egocentrism. At the same time, responsibilities to the wider community coexist with individual rights. For citizens of the young state to cooperate with the government, it was important that social cohesion be secured.

LEADERSHIP

To implement policy decisions, Singapore was fortunate to have a proactive government and a dedicated civil service made up of like-minded technocrats. These civil servants were committed to making economic growth a reality in the young and vulnerable city-state. To this end, political order was established through a very efficient and relatively incorrupt government. Meanwhile, political turbulence in the early years of independence and a desire to secure political stability pushed the PAP government to suppress destabilizing political opposition.[11] Foreign interference in domestic politics was strongly discouraged. Only constructive criticism from the media and opposition was accepted. Though often accused of being suppressive, government's principle was that wrong ideas or reportage must be challenged before they influence public opinion and create problems.[12]

The strategy to sustaining quality leadership was to choose the best man or woman for a specific task or project. As much as possible, a minister must be resourceful and have the ability to be innovative when faced with new, unexpected problems. Handing over to a new leadership was not taken lightly. Choice was not restricted to politicians. Viable candidates were sought from top echelons of all sectors (the professions, commerce, manufacturing and trade unions). Apart from having a disciplined mind, other qualities sought included courage, determination, commitment, character and the ability that makes people willing to follow.[13]

CONTROLLING CORRUPTION

From the day it took power, the PAP government resolved to chart a different path from that of corrupt leaders in neighbouring states. The government saw it as its mission to establish a clean and effective government. According to Lee Kuan Yew, Singaporeans expected purity in personal behaviour and in public life. To fulfil these expectations, government ensured that every dollar in revenue would be properly accounted for and would reach the beneficiaries at the grassroots without being siphoned along the way.[14]

A Corrupt Practices Investigation Bureau (CPIB) was mandated to investigate every officer and minister. The CPIB acquired a reputation for sniffing out those betraying public trust. Law enforcement agencies (Police and Immigration) and public service groups (hospital personnel) were also targeted for transformation. The CPIB was also competent to investigate corrupt practices in the private sector. Private companies were encouraged to report fraudulent kickbacks in private transactions. The leaders took it upon themselves to set a good example for civil servants. At the same time, the idea became sufficiently anchored in the Singaporean psyche due to what could be called a national ethical spirit.

Very high penalties are in place for transnational

bribery.[15] In 1989, the maximum fine for corruption was increased from S$10,000 to S$100,000. Giving false or misleading information to the CPIB became an offence subject to imprisonment and a fine of up to S$10,000. Courts were empowered to confiscate the benefits derived from corruption.[16]

Another measure to curb corruption entailed avoiding the use of monetary incentives to win elections and rather providing jobs in addition to social amenities. Ministers were also given adequate remuneration to reflect changing socio-economic conditions. Rather than underpaying ministers and adding incentives, the practice was to have all benefits expressed in a lump sum. This was meant to allow the ministers themselves to decide how to spend the money. Low incidence of corruption is believed to have contributed to Singapore's resiliency in the 1997 East Asian financial crisis.

ESTABLISHING THE RULE OF LAW

The government observed that the jury system did not have practical value for Singaporean society. Lee Kuan Yew was of the view that miscarriages of justice were prevalent because decisions were influenced by the vagaries of jury sentiments and superstitions. Government's principle was that a criminal is not a victim of society. The government settled on caning as being a more effective form of punishment for crimes (drugs, arms trafficking, rape, illegal entry and vandalizing of public property) than imposition of long prison terms. In 1997 Singapore was rated by the World Economic Forum's Global Competitiveness Report as a "country where organised crime does not impose significant costs on businesses." In the same year, the International Institute for Management Development rated Singapore number one for security, "where there is full confidence among people that their personal property is protected."[17]

From 1990, under Chief Justice Wee, **judicial reforms** were undertaken in Singapore. At the onset of the 1990s Singapore's judiciary was inefficient and inaccessible to many.[18] It was marked by common problems such as delays, high costs and antiquated methods. For a small country as Singapore, in 1991 for instance, the number of court cases pending included 30,000 criminal, 190,000 departmental and 40,000 traffic cases. This situation constituted a threat to the future of a rapidly growing economy as the state risked losing investors.

The ultimate goal of reforms was to modernize the judiciary for both economic and social growth. Focus areas included emphasis on raising the standards of the judiciary to enable Singapore to deal with the emerging challenges of globalization, technical advances and the impact of foreign cultures as well as knowledge.[19] The approach adopted was multidisciplinary and result-oriented.

To this end, Chief Justice Wee introduced fair and systematic methods of selecting judges. He introduced information technology (IT) into courts to speed up administrative work and court proceedings. Lawyers were able to file their court documents and make searches through their computers. Reforms were made participatory by broad publicizing of annual work plans and the opening of automated kiosks for obtaining information about legal services. Work plans set explicit markers for desired results and sharpened the judicial system's institutional image.[20] Strategic partnerships were formed with other organizations both locally and internationally, to improve the knowledge base.

Monitoring, evaluation and control of the modernization process and daily operations of courts was gradually institutionalized. By 1999, Singapore's courts had acquired a reputation that attracted visits by judges and chief justices from both developing and developed countries to study the reformation process.

ENSURING NATIONAL SECURITY

The security imperative was addressed by establishing a Ministry of Interior and Defence. The government was determined not to allow itself to be handicapped by any external intimidation. Instead, it believed that the important thing was not necessarily the size of the country's population (about 2 million at independence), but the fighting strength of its armed forces. It also saw the need to have a well educated and highly motivated army.

In partnership with consultants from Israel, the government decided to adopt a defence strategy based on the Israeli tactic of mobilizing the maximum number of people in the shortest possible time. To this end, a five-year plan was drawn envisaging the mobilization and training of 250,000 Singaporeans between the ages of 18 and 35. One hundred and fifty thousand (150,000) of them were to be drawn from the reserve service whilst older people and women were to be recruited for non-combatant duties. By January 1968, the government had purchased French-made AMV 13 light tanks from Israelis at discount prices. In 1969, 72 refurbished tanks and 170 four-wheeled V 200 armoured vehicles were purchased.[21]

In efforts to involve the entire population in a "total defence" concept, a ten-year plan was also drawn to reorient the people (especially the Chinese) to overcome their traditional dislike for soldiering. Cadet corps were formed in schools and National Service became a rite of passage for the young men. Involving the entire population in a security policy helped to unify Singapore's heterogeneous society. By 1990, the Singapore Armed Forces had acquired the reputation of a respected and professional force capable of defending the territorial integrity and independence of the state.

SOCIAL DEVELOPMENT

One of Government's greatest challenges was to achieve social cohesion within a heterogeneous society. This was achieved by creating equal opportunities for all, regardless of race. Government eventually realized the importance of appreciating the unique abilities of each race (Chinese, Indian and Malay) and encouraging them to work in fields in which they were most efficient.

EDUCATION

The government emphasised individual competition rather than inherited status. This made education a highly valued asset in Singapore society since it was seen as the key to upward social mobility. Indeed, the government believed that talent is a country's most precious asset. Government also recognised that the more talented people there were as government ministers, administrators and professionals, the more effective the policies, the better the results.

Singapore was fortunate to have been the regional centre for education during British rule. The government thus took advantage of the availability of educational institutions and encouraged citizens to pursue education with all seriousness. Women were encouraged to pursue higher education. Both graduate and non-graduate men were encouraged to marry graduate women (and vice versa) in a bid to have a generation of Singaporean children with higher intelligence quotients (IQs).[22]

Education played an important role in engendering significant poverty reduction. This was partly due to an increased participation of women in the workforce and the resultant increase in the number of wage-earners in families. This translated into improvement in the material circumstances of households. Household income distribution in Singapore from 1982 to 1983 was roughly equivalent to that of the United Kingdom, though the latter emphasised individualistic rather than communitarian values. Poverty fell from 19% of households in 1953-1954 to 0.3% in 1982-1983.[23]

TACKLING BRAIN DRAIN

As a small state, Singapore has to make extra efforts to attract and retain as many talented and qualified people as possible. The country's talent pool challenges were aggravated when rich Western countries changed policies on Asian immigration. Singapore lost professionals to America, Canada, Australia, New Zealand and Britain. To get enough qualified persons to fill jobs in the growing economy, the government decided to carry out a systematic search for talent worldwide.

This was done through Singapore's missions abroad.

Asian graduates were offered recruitment opportunities in Singapore. Scholarships were also offered to Asian students. The rationale behind targeting Asians was that Singapore offered an Asian society with a higher standard of living and quality of life than those of the students. It was assumed that they could also assimilate easily into Singaporean society. An annual inflow of a few hundred made up for the loss through emigration of 5-10 percent of Singaporean professionals. By the 1990s, however, the inflow of professionals through active recruitment was 3 times the outflow.[24]

STANDARDS OF LIVING

The PAP government's policy was to create a fair society rather than one of welfare in character. The plan was to even out extreme results of free market competition by redistributing the national income through subsidies on things that improved the earning power of citizens. After observing the welfare systems of Britain and Sweden, the PAP government concluded that welfare increased government expenditure and undermined self-reliance.

Lee Kuan Yew believed that people who had substantial savings had a different attitude to life. Such people tended to be more responsible for themselves and their families. Singaporeans were thus encouraged to adopt a saving culture that would help them become self-reliant. Each generation was to pay for itself and each individual was to save towards his or her own future (home, health and pension).[25]

The government rigorously pursued a *home-owning policy* in which urban dwellers (civilian and military alike) owned their own homes. In 1968 the government launched a revised home ownership scheme under the Home Development Board (HDB). Each citizen was to increase contributions to a compulsory savings scheme known as the Central Provident Fund. The scheme was sustained by effecting a corresponding increase in contributions based on annual salary increases. Taking cognisance of the limited land in Singapore, the government built high-rise apartments. The architecture varied depending on the landscape. To prevent older homes from looking like slums, they were refurbished to match the standards of newer estates.

HEALTH

Upon considering the limitations in the British National Health Service scheme and the American style medical insurance schemes, the government decided to find a different solution for Singapore. The health policy entailed the provision of good health services with wastage and unplanned costs kept in check by requiring co-payments from the user.

ECONOMIC DEVELOPMENT

Cho-oon asserts that economic policy in Singapore is characterized by "pragmatism."[26] This is to say that the economy has been shepherded along by the state surmounting one challenge at a time. Policies were pragmatic in the sense that rather than follow rigid principles, policies were implemented in a spirit of willingness to adapt and change according to what circumstances require. In view of her economic circumstances, Singapore adopted an outward-oriented industrialization strategy to address her state-specific economic needs. The economic policy was highly interventionist or state-led. This found expression in the provision of fiscal and financial incentives and the establishment of state-owned enterprises. There was also extensive intervention in the labour market and heavy reliance on FDI. In the absence of a regional common market, Singapore found her new hinterland in America, Europe and Japan.

INDUSTRIALIZATION

Given the post-independence challenges, industrialization was seen to be the panacea to unemployment and economic survival. Efforts were enhanced with the establishment of the Singapore Tourist Promotion Board and the opening of factories. The initial industrialization plan focused on fields that were not found in neighbouring countries. Singapore had a comparative advantage in labour-intensive heavy industry, especially in the areas of shipbuilding and the processing of oil products.

From 1979 to 1981 new industrialization policies were adopted owing to growing competition from neighbouring countries and the rising cost of doing business in Singapore. New priority economic sectors identified include precision engineering, electronics, information technology, optics, chemicals, pharmaceuticals, aeronautics, telecommunications and biotechnology.[27]

TRADE AND INVESTMENT

Far from buying the dependency school's assertion that MNCs had neo-colonialist motives, the government's investment policy was biased in favour of foreign investors. This was especially since the local entrepreneurial sector was weak. The government proceeded to create a conducive investment climate for investors. It built the infrastructure, provided well-planned industrial estates, equity participation in industries and sound macroeconomic policies essential to enable successful private enterprise operation. In 1967, a comprehensive Economic Expansion Act was introduced to replace earlier investment ordinances. The aim was to accelerate depreciation and to allow duty-free import of required equipment inputs.

The government's approach to managing multinational companies played a key role in shaping policy decisions and in nurturing large state-owned companies run by the civil service bureaucracy. Together, state enterprises and MNCs provided the main thrust for economic development.

Investment efforts were facilitated by the Economic Development Board. Its role was to serve as a one-stop agency that saved the investor the trouble of having to deal with a large number of departments and ministries. The Board's role in attracting a steady flow of ever higher value-added investments enabled Singapore to remain competitive in spite of rising wages and business costs. In 1997 for instance, Singapore had almost 200 American manufacturing companies worth more than $19 billion of investments at book value.[28]

To further enhance export oriented investment, Singapore (though still a Third World Country) proceeded to create an international financial centre in 1968. The plan was to take up banking services after San Francisco closed in the afternoon to enable an unprecedented 24-hour round-the-world service in money and banking. The Monetary Authority of Singapore provided professional financial supervision, operating according to laws, rules and regulations. These were periodically reviewed and revised to keep pace with developments in financial services.

Singapore suffered a recession in the early 1980s but recovered relatively quickly. A 1977 report by the Chinese Chamber of Commerce and Industry had revealed that the EDB's intense promotion of foreign investors and direct competition from government companies were causing local businessmen to be squeezed on both sides. To address this issue, the government announced a change of policy in 1985. Government would start up new industries only in cases where support for private entrepreneurs was indispensable. Privatisation was also considered by the government.

LABOUR RELATIONS

To attract and keep investors, as well as maximize productivity, it was indispensable that the political climate be regulated and that there be predictability and stability in the pattern of industrial relations. Statistics indicate that the latter issue was addressed in an efficacious manner. From 1965, the government intensified its control of labour conduct, increasingly aligning efforts with the development agenda. The National Trades Union Congress (NTUC) was made to operate in line with a "Charter for Industrial Progress" that was based on "cooperative labour-management relations." The number of work stoppages reduced from 161 in 1961 to zero in 1969.[29]

The Government sought to promote attitudinal change in the labour industry. There was the need to educate union leaders and workers on the importance of attracting investments for such a young and vulnerable state. Workers were made to understand that pay must accord with performance, not time spent on the job. Triple pay for work on public holidays was abolished. Strikes were banned in certain essential services. A change in union culture was further triggered following the deregistration of two influential labour unions in January 1967. From thence, demands shifted from defiant flouting of laws to that of reasonable give-and-take negotiations.

The aim of the new labour laws was to boost the confidence of employers (especially those of multinational companies) in Singaporean workers. Another goal was to demonstrate that labour in Singapore was disciplined and provided a low-cost resource. It may appear that government-labour relations were rather oppressive. However, government also took up the responsibility of promoting labour interests. The approach to managing employer-labour relations was corporatist rather than legalistic.

Employers were entreated to be fair to their workers if they wanted optimal efforts from them. Wage levels were regulated through a National Wages Council in consultation with all stakeholders. Government was prepared to provide individual returns by way of homes, health, education and social benefits. Under the leadership of Devan Nair (1970-1981) NTUC leaders were educated on basic economic principles and encouraged to face challenges in world markets by modernizing trade union functions. A number of union cooperative enterprises were set up to lower the cost of living for members. To sustain good labour relations efforts, an Institute of Labour Studies was established in 1990 to offer programmes in industrial relations and leadership development.[30]

THE ISSUE OF AID

The PAP government was determined to inculcate an attitude of self-dependence rather than aid-dependence in Singaporeans. In a message to Singaporean workers, Lee Kuan Yew stated that, "the world does not owe us a living. We cannot live by the begging bowl."[31]

British military withdrawal between 1968 and 1971 threatened to destabilize the Singapore economy. The state lost about 20% GDP that had previously provided 30,000 jobs in direct employment and another 40,000 in support services. Yet, the government refused to operate on regular injections of relief proposed by the British government. Instead, the PAP government would only accept assistance that would provide Singaporeans with jobs through industries. To this end, negotiations were concluded in March 1968 with a £50 million aid package to be spent on goods and services, with 25% in grants and 75% in loans. The government spent half on development projects and the other on British defence equipment. By the time the withdrawal was completed, there was no unemployment as the 30,000 retrenched workers were absorbed by industries. In addition to this, no land or building was left idle or derelict.[32]

Another factor that helped the government to avoid foreign borrowing was its welfare policy which discouraged wasteful expenditure. The system was sustained through monetary stability, a balanced budget, low taxes, ample investments and high productivity. This kept inflation low. Additional voluntary savings in a Post Office Savings Bank (POSBANK) helped the government to pay for infrastructure including roads, bridges, airports, container ports, power stations, reservoirs, and a mass rapid transport system. A guiding principle for every minister of finance over the years has been to avoid spending more than is collected in revenue. Sustained growth in Singapore has thus been achieved through a pattern of low expenditure – high savings – low welfare – high investments. This has contributed to stability in the country.

ENVIRONMENTAL CONSIDERATIONS VERSUS ATTITUDINAL CHANGE

As part of the growth strategy to create a First World Oasis in a Third World Region, the government decided to transform Singapore into a tropical city. The aim was to provide First World standards to attract business people and tourists. This was achieved by no easy means. The government soon realised that it was easier to improve physical infrastructure than to change ingrained habits of a people. Citizen participation in these efforts was promoted through education and sensitisation.

It took years for the government to succeed in clearing the streets of illegal hawkers and pirate taxi drivers (unlicensed and without insurance cover). Law was enforced only after many jobs had been created and hawkers had been resettled. Other developments included tree planting, appointment of research teams, cleaning of the Singapore River to increase portable water supply, creation of a beach along the banks of the Kallang Basin and establishment of strict antipollution standards. To save the younger generation of Singaporeans from health hazards, smoking was banned in public places. Regardless of ridicule from some developed countries, the sale and use of chewing gum were also eventually banned in 1992. Discipline in all these areas was established through education, persuasion and winning over the majority and then establishing legislation to punish the wilful minority that was unprepared to cooperate.[33]

SINGAPORE IN THE NEW MILLENNIUM: 2000-2005

The government continued to play a very active role in the drive towards growth and in controlling social behaviour. Policing of the outer boundaries of the state was done to keep out illegal immigration. While the economy was largely liberalized, all factors of production crossing into or out of the territory were kept under strict control.[34] Having progressively chalked up successes over the years from primary through to tertiary sectors, Singapore appeared to be focusing more on the quaternary sector. Two main fields included Information Technology and Research and Development.

Research and Development (R&D) is a field in which research professionals engage in the conception or creation of new knowledge, products, processes, methods and systems. They also conduct systematic management of projects concerned. A report by the Singapore Agency for Science, Technology and Development indicated that gross expenditure on R&D (GERD) increased from S$3.0 billion in 2000 to $4.6 billion in 2005. This 8.8% increase was driven by both the private and public sectors. As a percentage of GDP, GERD rose from 1.9% in 2000 to 2.4% in 2005. In the same period, the number of researchers increased from

19,551 to 27,969. With GERD at 2.4% of GDP in 2005, Singapore's R&D intensity was ahead of the EU's 1.9% but lower than those of USA (2.7) and Japan (3.2).[35]

In the 40th year of independence, statistics indicated a Singaporean society that had generally adapted well to trends in globalisation. A report by Infocomm Development Authority of Singapore revealed a significant increase in internet usage by individuals and households. [36] The implication was that Singaporeans were increasingly becoming IT-literate. Statistics in this same report indicated a socio-economic climate for high standards of living:

- Population: 4.35 million
- Average life expectancy at birth: 78 years for males and 82 years for females
- Literacy rate: 97.4% for males and 92.7% for females
- Per capita gross national income: S$44,455
- Official foreign reserves: S$194 billion
- Mobile phone subscribers: 978 per 1,000 people
- Residential broadband subscribers: 162 per 1,000 resident population.

Conclusion

From the above discussion, it is evident that within 40 years of independence Singapore had come a long way in surviving as a small city-state within a region of few industrialized countries. The government's strategy for maintaining high productivity was to plan broad economic objectives and set targets for project completion. Plans were regularly reviewed and adjusted as new realities changed the outlook. Providing infrastructure and the training of workers to meet the needs of employers were planned years in advance. Promoting attitudinal change and enforcing discipline played an equally important role.

The next chapter provides a contrasting picture of Africa, a largely Third World continent still waddling in developmental challenges. The second part of the chapter outlines major lessons that can be drawn from the Singapore model.

CHAPTER TWO

AFRICAN DEVELOPMENTAL CHALLENGES

The current international system may be dominated by Western precepts and Africa may have been forced into the world capitalist climate through colonialism. These facts notwithstanding, the truth is that the meaning and essence of development is by no means alien to Africa.[1] The reality is that African citizens demand development because it defines their past, present and future quality of life. Certainly, countless have been the controversies surrounding the definition of development. None-the-less, at the end of the day the primary object is the person, his/her well-being and enhancement of his/her creative potentials.

Eghosa Osaghae observes that Africa has wide diversities in her development experience in terms of history, autonomous institutions and practices, colonial legacies, socioeconomic and political capacities, world views and structural processes.[2] Yet the continent, especially the sub-Saharan region, shares some common experiences. These territories were victims of dehumanizing effects of the slave trade as well as colonial ravages and exploitations.

Independence from colonial rule and foreign domination bore a promise and hope that Africans will be masters of their own destiny and fulfil their aspirations for a better life. This dream was however short-lived. Postcolonial history is replete with forms of governance that proved detrimental to progress.[3] The picture was that of corruption, maladministration, poor management of resources, rising debt, human rights abuses, military coups, needless conflicts and sometimes anarchy. Africa became the 'sick' continent with an image of famine, diseases and war-torn societies that defied trade and investment, technological advancement and the quest for progress and development.

Subsequently, over fifty years after independence, instead of being liberated from the shackles of underdevelopment in its political, social and economic dimensions, Africa finds herself at the bottom of the league of development in the world. These failures have been largely attributed to poor governance. Vladimir Antwi Danso provides a clear picture of the nature of governance in Africa:

"Africa is known to have produced some of the most grotesquely inept, corrupt and predatory governments in the world, especially in the second half of the Twentieth Century. Most African leaders have been exclusivist, imprudent in economic management, profligate, corrupt and dictatorial… In such a setting state capacity to sustain itself is eroded and in most places implosion sets in."[4]

Osaghae identifies three broad class strata in the African societal structure. The first is the privileged or bourgeois class comprising the minority ruling class. This group consists of those who actually control the reins of government and political power (politicians, military officers, bureaucrats and the intelligentsia, as well as their private sector counterparts). The second class is the working class in both the public and private sectors, including the self-employed. The third class is the peripheral class consisting of peasants and other peripheral groups.[5]

Osaghae is of the view that the African predicament can be explained by both external and internal factors.[6] Colonialism is identified as an experience that took the development initiative from Africa. It follows that Africans have since been at the receiving end of imposed development paradigms over which they exercise no control.

The African predicament exists largely because the state and citizens have divergent perceptions on what development really means. While citizens look inward for self-help solutions, external forces largely influence government policies. Although citizens have formed self-help groups over the years, they remain largely dependent on government to provide employment, education, health and basic infrastructural facilities.[7] As far as Africans are concerned government is capable of improving their quality of life only if it would review its priorities to favour the people.

EFFORTS TO IMPROVE THE AFRICAN CONDITION

Osaghae identifies the Lagos Plan of Action (LPA), 1981, to be the first major attempt by government to be the first major attempt by government to reconcile the opposing perceptions on development.[8] This framework proposed a shift from externally oriented development strategies to self-reliance. In addition was self-sustained development at the national and regional levels. However, this vision was dead at birth as the Structural Adjustment Programme soon took over the realm of affairs.

Onimode gives a list of indigenous development strategies since the 1980s.[9] These include (a) Human or people oriented development, a strategy aimed at putting the people first; (b) The AAF-SAP, designed by the Economic Commission for Africa (ECA); (c) The LPA; (d) Participatory Development, aimed at democratising the development process; (e) Bottom-up development, promoting ownership of development strategies at the grassroots level; (f) Sustainable Development, aimed at making the development process self-sustaining rather than dependent on foreign aid; (g) South Africa's Reconstruction and Development Programme, perceived to be the boldest practical project for an African Renaissance.

According to Mbaya Kankwenda, Africa's development agenda for the Twenty First Century include the following: (a) building peace and political and social stability; (b) promoting sustained, endogenous and equitable economic growth; (c) improving the well-being of the population and the ending of human poverty.[10]

Apart from the above-mentioned strategies, S.K.B. Asante identifies the promotion of regional economic integration as a widely recognized and necessary condition for the long-term sustainable development of African countries.[11] He is also of the view that it is one of the most potent strategies for facing up to globalization and for redressing the socio-economic situation of the continent.

Various African governments have also adopted the Millennium Development Goals (MDGs) spearheaded by the United Nations Organisation (UNO) as a promising scheme for improving the quality of life for Africans.

These efforts are certainly noble and the ideas appear to be excellent, but what prevents Africa from actually being able to implement programmes in a sustainable manner to foster progress? It is interesting to note that the government of Ghana for instance seems to have drawn some inspiration from Singapore. A national reorientation programme was launched in 2007, but not much progress has been made. African governments and scholars seem to be quick to come up with development objectives. But the implementation process or *how* to get to the destination is usually the problem. For how long is Africa going to be a buyer of development paradigms?

THE AFRICAN CHALLENGE

Twenty-two years ago Philip Ndegwa attempted to examine the problem of underdevelopment in Africa by conducting an in-depth analysis of what exactly is wrong with Africa.[12] It will be observed that what he terms the *African Challenge*, is still as relevant today as it was over twenty years ago. Sadly little has changed. The challenges are self-repeating. Ndegwa outlined a number of challenges.

Challenge 1: How to survive as autonomous countries

Taking cognisance of the fact that there is a direct link between economic viability and political stability, the combined effect of poor leadership and economic failure has often led to weak and politically volatile states. The consequence is continued dependence on foreign assistance in areas of food supply and military support. The author predicted loss of national cohesion and disintegration of states.[13] Chad, Sudan and Angola were cited as such affected states. Sad to say, political instability remains, especially in the first two states.

Challenge 2: How to manage and develop valuable resources for the benefit of all Africans

Africa is one of the richest continents in terms of natural resources. It is endowed with 97% of the world's chrome, 85% of its platinum, 70-80% its gold and diamonds, 64% of manganese. Other resources include copper, cobalt, uranium, oil and natural gas. The continent also has at least 25% of the world's power potential.[14] Yet Africa has not succeeded in balancing the share of Transnational and Multinational corporations to control the exploitation of her resources.

Challenge 3: How to sustain the environment

This challenge comes largely as a result of increasing pressures on land resources due to rising populations. Availability of arable land, erosion and climate change are also contributing factors.

Challenge 4: How to shift from aid-dependence to self-sufficiency

Africa still struggles to find a balance between attracting and managing capital for development through investment and aid. It is often argued that it is unfair to compare Africa to the Asian Tigers because the latter received huge sums of foreign aid to kick-start the development process. But the critical question to ask is: "what would have happened to this same amount of money if it had fallen into the hands of African governments?" Would the money have been invested in the projects that demand urgent attention? Will the ordinary African citizen have enjoyed any benefits accruing?

Challenge 5: How to apply accumulated knowledge and experience in dealing with the economic, social and scientific problems in development

African scholars and policymakers are yet to find concrete answers to the following questions: (a) How can the right development paradigm be identified? (b) How can proposed strategies be re-examined or analysed in an objective manner to avoid pitfalls? (c) How can officials know which advice from foreign experts to accept and which to reject? (d) How best can domestic policy be planned to be well adapted to the international climate? (e) How can a more rapid implementation of development paradigms be ensured? (f) How best can plans be adjusted to reflect changing local and international conditions?

Challenge 6: How to build appropriate political, social and economic institutions at the national, regional and continental levels to increase efficiency and productivity

African governments are yet to appropriately address the following questions: (a) To what extent should government involve itself in the provision of goods and services? (b) To what extent should the private sector be involved in the development process? (c) How best can the political machinery be organised to ensure good governance? (d) Does the western professed multi-party democracy necessarily ensure more efficient governance?

S.K.B Asante draws attention to the critical issue of building the human resource capacity of Africa. He posits that integration schemes in Africa and various development goals have not achieved set goals due to the absence of external intellectual, technical and professional inputs underpinning the efforts of governments and their inter-governmental organizations.[15] In other words politicians cannot handle the task alone. Experts, technocrats and the private sector are needed to enhance capacity building.

Challenge 7: How to promote Attitudinal Change

This is an issue that Ndegwa did not devote much attention to, but which is more or less a determinant to Africa's future. For how long are Africans going to view themselves as somewhat inferior to the descendants of their colonial masters? Today this inferiority complex seems to have spread towards Asians and South Americans (or for that matter any fair-skinned race). How to develop a positive and can-do-it attitude to development thus remains a major challenge for African governments and citizens alike.

Indeed, in a recent lecture organised in Accra, Ghana, by the Institute of Democratic Governance (IDEG) and the African Centre for Economic Transformation (ACET), Prof. Stiglitz (a Noble Prize Laureate in Economics) confirmed most of these challenges.[16] He lamented that Africa's resources are given away in return for pittance. He also touched on the challenge of unfavourable terms of trade. He implored the state to play a catalytic role in bringing about structural transformation for economic growth. Stiglitz's lecture on drawing lessons from Asia ushers the discussions into the second part of this chapter on lessons from Singapore.

CHAPTER THREE

LESSONS FROM SINGAPORE

Deciding on an appropriate development strategy can be one of the most challenging tasks for any government – whether democratic or otherwise. Since development is a multidimensional process, the need to pay attention to detail cannot be overemphasised. The ability to plan and actually implement programmes is an art in itself. This chapter calls for Africa, and for that matter, other Developing Countries to adopt a pragmatic approach to development. It is not the size of the country per se, but the ability to manage natural resources and develop human capacity that counts. While it is accepted that every project cannot be undertaken at the same time, it is equally important that countries adjust quickly to changing circumstances. According to the Late Kofi Annan (former Secretary-General of the United Nations) Singapore will be of great interest to people of other developing countries and to all those who are interested in their fate.[1]

The increase beyond a certain GDP per capita figure is what prompted the World Bank to officially classify Singapore as a "developed economy."[2] However, behind the numbers is a distinct story of a nation that fought with great determination and integrity for its mere survival before prosperity was a possibility.[3] Singapore paid attention to detail or the simple factors that could undermine progress and worked on finding practical solutions. The leaders took into consideration the fact that development theories can be complicated and sometimes impractical. The lessons are discussed along the lines of factors contributing to the African challenge. The issues are by no means exhaustive.

Lesson 1: To survive as an autonomous country requires patriotism, confidence and preparedness to take risks.

Singapore's exit from Malaysia was a unique historical situation. However, her problems at independence were not unique. High levels of unemployment, lack of sanitation, little supply of potable water, and ethnic conflict were conditions that marred Singapore then and still characterize many Third World countries today.[4] There was every indication for Singaporeans to give up and allow themselves to waddle in the sea of hopelessness (as has become the fate of some African countries). However, this was Lee Kuan Yew's response to foreign pessimists at independence:

"Don't worry about Singapore. My colleagues and I are

sane and rational people even in our moments of anguish. We weigh all possible consequences before we make any move on the political chess board . . . our people have the will to fight and the stuff that makes for survival."[5]

The political and economic conditions in the early days may have been dire, but the quick and decisive actions of its leaders throughout its development have rarely been matched elsewhere. Early Singaporean leaders knew exactly what they wanted. They had concrete long-term plans in place so that no nation could impose directives on them. This attitude helped create foreign confidence in the Singaporean government. Indeed during deliberations concerning the pull out of the British military, the British government "bent over backward to help" bring about the best solution.[6] They even made proposals for growth strategies. But the PAP government did not think agriculture or light industry very promising for the young state. Instead, it confidently turned to export-led growth.

Singapore's survival experience is indicative of the fact that the supposed Western enemies can do little to harm a state if the state knows what it wants and is bold enough to pursue it. A state's self-confidence wins the respect of foreign states. A helpless and uncertain attitude, on the other hand, only opens doors for foreign interference. At the same time, confidence means little when, like Mugabe's Zimbabwe, confidence translates into a refusal to respond to constructive criticism. The confidence must come out of a determination to lead the country into greener pastures – not into a bottomless pit.

Lesson 2: Valuable resources can benefit all citizens as long as they are prudently managed and fairly distributed.

Conventional wisdom in economics in the 1960s held that every industrialized nation, especially a small one, needed a hinterland to succeed. Singapore had none.[7] Neither was she endowed with the kind of natural resources found in other regions of the world, especially Africa.

The best Singapore could do in such circumstances was to look out and wide for opportunities it could get. The city-state had to link up with the developed world and attract their manufacturers to produce in Singapore and export their products to the developed countries.[8]

One may argue that it was these same MNCs and TNCs who overexploited Africa's natural resources, leaving abject poverty in their wake. The truth is that, unlike many African governments, the Singapore government exercised considerable discipline in managing the country's economic affairs. Appropriate laws were in place to ensure that foreign companies did not take undue advantage of the small city-state. In addition to concrete laws, the investment environment in Singapore was such that foreign companies were confident that their businesses will thrive and hence had no cause to engage in corrupt practices. This is not to say that laws are not in place in developing countries. The problem is that implementation is poor. Sometimes the benefits derived from the foreign companies fall into the pockets of the government officials themselves rather than into the national coffers. This brings us to the issue of how corruption alone has the potential to squander a nation's resources.

Arvis et.al. observe that the clear determination of Singapore's political leaders to weed out corruption was the key to the state's success in implementing good governance and a strong anticorruption ethos.[9] Government's ability to rally public support was a powerful tool for combating corruption. In 1987, Prime Minister Lee Kuan Yew told parliament that the strongest deterrent is in a public opinion which censures and condemns corrupt persons.

The law not only severely punishes corruption in Singapore, but it does so strictly and swiftly. This acts as a real deterrent to both Singaporean nationals and foreigners living and working in Singapore. Prosecution is non-discriminatory in both low-level and high profile cases. The major challenge is to ensure that Singaporean companies in foreign countries (perhaps where laws are less strict) still maintain high standards of anti-corruption culture.

Another resource management measure entailed carefully prioritising economic planning and implementation of each plan at stages over a targeted period. This was done to avoid inflation, the risk of devaluation, or balance of payment problems. In doing so, the state held substantial amounts of official reserves even while being an underdeveloped country with its economy in great need for public spending. This discipline was held in good times and bad. Thus, Singapore "stood out as an island of stability in a sea of disparity" when the Asian economic crisis struck in 1997.[10] Conversely, the economies of her neighbours collapsed under huge amounts of short-term debt borrowed in foreign currency.

In addition to this, Singaporean government, economists, researchers and businessmen were innovative enough to diversify rather than stick only to old methods of production. This yielded positive results for the economy. Africa, on the other hand, continues to stick to methods of production adopted in the colonial days.

Lesson 3: The importance government attaches to its human resources and the investments it makes in its own people determine the success of any development vision. This strategy can help build a confident people and subsequently contribute greatly to a shift from aid-dependence to self-sufficiency.

In the midst of post-independence trials, the government

made it a point to offer the people hope rather than demoralize them. The social contract that was articulated between the ruling PAP-run government and the people of Singapore was another defining factor in the state's approach to development. Basically the terms were that while the people were willing to accept more government control, give up some individual rights, and work hard, the government would create the environment that would deliver prosperity and a better quality of life.[11]

This strategy has been based on the realization that in the long run, it is skilled and highly motivated people who improve economic efficiency and thus produce economic growth. It is talented individuals at work who allow Singapore, an island which even has to import its water, to run a GDP per capita roughly 25 times that of Iran, a country liberally endowed with petroleum, natural gas and other minerals.[12]

In addition to rich human resource, adopting a savings culture is essential for reducing aid-dependence. The government later liberalized the CPF to allow investment in private, commercial and industrial properties, as well as trustee shares, unit trusts or mutual funds. Making citizens caretakers of their own destinies make them more mature, responsible and less dependent on government. At the same time the PAP government did not lose sight of the fact that there will always be a small percentage of irresponsible or incapable people in society.

Raising employee morale is another strategy to enriching a state's human resource base. The cooperative enterprises (health services, child care, seaside resort, country club, hotel etc.) into which the NTUC invested, served to greatly boost the morale of public servants. The facilities helped improve the lifestyles of workers and helped reduce the feeling that they belonged to a lower grade of workers who could not enjoy such services.[13] The enterprises also gave more union leaders hands-on experience in running businesses.

The positive attitude with which the NTUC approached the enterprises not only helped to increase wages, but also created jobs. Unemployment reduced from 14% in 1965 to 1.8% in 1997.[14] Employee satisfaction must have contributed much to reduce corruption.

African government workers, on the other hand, cannot boast of such golden opportunities. Work ethics is poor. Nepotism and favouritism has placed square pegs in round holes. Conditions of service are poor. Employee morale is often low and translates into low productivity.

Lesson 4: Pragmatism must be applied to accumulated knowledge and experience in order to deal effectively with the economic, social and scientific problems in development.

In as much as Singaporean ministers and public servants

were well educated, they were constantly seeking to broaden their knowledge base. Their practice was to observe how other states had addressed their development issues. The next step was to decide which successful experiences to adopt for Singapore and which mistakes to avoid. Government did not allow itself to be imprisoned by theories, but rather be guided by reason and reality. The practice was to apply what Lee Kuan Yew terms the acid test to every theory and every scheme. The key question was, "would it work (for Singapore)?"[15]

Additionally, problem solving also has to do with ability to learn from mistakes and move on. Government projects must be carried out realistically. The PAP government learnt a bitter lesson that it does not pay to yield to popular pressure beyond government capacity to deliver.[16] Between 1982 and 1984, in response to increasing demand for apartments, an ambitious attempt by government to more than double the building of apartments turned out to be disastrous. Workmen ended up being overstretched. This in turn decreased the quality of the buildings. Renovations to rectify the situation were carried out in later years at a great cost to government. But the lesson was worth learning in order to avoid mistakes in the future.

It is undeniable that, governments are bound to make mistakes and encounter problems. It is not enough to have the best of talented people in charge of the state. It is their ability to surmount challenges that determines success. Sadly governments of developing countries tend to leave things as they are until the situation is beyond repair and lives are in jeopardy, then a state of emergency is declared.

Lesson 5: The commitment of a state's leadership is key to building appropriate political, social and economic institutions to increase efficiency and productivity.

Being elected to office by the general populace provides no guarantee that national leaders will be free of corruption, effective, or dedicated to the national interest. Governments are often rejected because they betray the peoples' trust. It is easy to start off with high moral standards, strong convictions and determination to improve conditions in society but without strong and determined leaders, it would be difficult to live up to such good intentions. At the same time adequate remuneration is vital for promoting high standards of probity in political leaders and high officials.

Singapore's leadership worked hard to maintain a culture of team spirit and unflinching commitment to the cause of the state. They saw running a government as similar to that of conducting an orchestra so that each minister put in his or her best to ensure that harmony was achieved in development efforts.[17] Differences on policies were kept within cabinet until solutions are found and a consensus reached. The same cannot be said of African politicians. Rather than build up team spirit, individuals and groups of politicians undermine each other's efforts. Even innocent policies are politicised and public opinion is poisoned. In the end, neither politicians nor citizens are willing to cooperate with government efforts.

In observing Singapore's political, social and economic institutions, it can be posited that what moves institutions forward is not so much upgrading facilities, but a deliberate drive towards changing the institutional culture as a whole. The attitude of Singaporean bureaucrats at independence was not much different from those of developing countries, yet through reforms positive results were reaped.

The judicial reforms in Singapore may be applicable to other government institutions. Waleed Haider drew the following lessons from his research on Singapore's judicial reforms:

Strategic thinking and business planning are central to institutional success. Reformers must thus adopt a holistic and participatory approach to foster teamwork at all levels.

Strong leadership is essential in creating and achieving a vision of change. In other words, a strong leader is indispensable for motivating and directing the reform process.

Institutional reforms must be tailored for and targeted at those whom the institution serves. Reforms must meet the needs of specific beneficiaries.

Knowledge and technical innovation are critical components of change. This may be done through personnel training, knowledge sharing and information technology.[18]

Democracy does not necessarily guarantee the best system of governance. Although Singapore's communitarian system played an important role in fostering social stability and economic growth, the system is often criticized as being coercive and depriving the populace of involvement in the decision making process. However, in reality the system seems to grant citizens the privilege of getting the government to meet their needs.[19] Voting in Singapore tends to register citizens' dissatisfaction with government policies and to express expectations rather than to oust a government. Hence, rather than it making government a dictatorship, the communitarian approach keeps leaders constantly alert to citizens' expectations. The ruling party is in a constant process of reworking its legitimising ideology to suit changing economic circumstances. This could explain Singapore's adaptability to a rapidly changing world.

African governments, on the other hand tend to become complacent after a short time of being in power. Many African countries have adopted democracy but substantial growth has not been evident. Elections are also often marked with violence. Elections neither succeed in ousting inefficient governments nor pushing them to improve policies. Some have been in power for almost four decades and have lost innovativeness but have no intention of leaving the position to give way for a new generation of leaders. Hence, the effectiveness of any system of government depends on the incumbent government's commitment to reap positive results for the people.

Closely related to the issue of elections is the fact that, the attitude of past governments towards new governments is an art of state building in itself. It determines the future prospects of a state. Recognizing this fact, the PAP government attached a lot of importance to passing on the baton to new leaders. What the outgoing government was interested in was not personal gain but rather what was best for the future of the country. For this reason, the government made sure that the right people were found to fill positions. Rather than undermine the efforts of the next generation of leaders, the past leaders derived immense satisfaction in offering constructive advice and watching them gain confidence in their new posts. Indeed Lee Kuan Yew observed that the second generation of leaders brought a fresh burst of energy and enthusiasm into the government. Furthermore, their experiences and ideas were more in tune with the younger generation of Singaporeans and they were better poised to lead the country into the new millennium.[20]

To render effective development efforts, law enforcement agencies must play a critical role to ensure order, peace and stability. It goes without saying that the Army and Police must be seen as protectors rather than symbols of coercion. As long as law enforcement workers are offered good incentives or good conditions of service, it is easier for the government to win and maintain their loyalty as well as build their motivation. Singapore's government, for instance, had a policy that all who enlisted in the SAF as full time career people would be guaranteed jobs in government, statutory boards, or the private sector when they left full service.[21] Against a different background, deplorable conditions of service for the military and police have often resulted in dissatisfaction, demotivation, rebellions, coups, lawlessness, and human rights abuses in Africa.

On the social front, a fair and even-handed policy promotes harmony among various races in society. In Singapore, costs and benefits were shared evenly among majority and minority alike. The law was also enforced impartially, regardless of race or religion. In addition to this was the question of which language to choose as the official language. Singapore's choice of English as the working language not only prevented conflict between the different races, but also gave the state a competitive advantage. This is because English is the international language of business and diplomacy, science and technology.[22] It was a question of practicality, not race. The devastations of social unrest and bloody wars that Africa has experienced as a result of government failure to adequately address delicate issues of ethnicity still haunt the continent.

Thanks to well organized institutions, highly qualified and dedicated public servants as well as a marked desire for excellence, the effectiveness of the Singapore government has been rather unusual. This has won the small state worldwide acclaim over the years. The Institute of Management Development's World Competitiveness Yearbook 1997, ranked Singapore as the country most effective and fastest at implementing changes in government policy.[23]

Lesson 6: Changing the ingrained attitudes of a people is perhaps one of the most daunting tasks for any society; but with practical laws and effective implementation, such a task can be accomplished.

Lee Kuan Yew observed that it could take generations to change the lifestyles and cultural inclinations of a people. He recounted a rather comic situation of how long it took Singaporean farmers to recover from the cultural shock of moving from their farms into high-rise buildings. Some insisted on keeping their animals in their rooms. Others continued to use their traditional lanterns instead of making use of the available electricity. It is interesting to note that early Singaporeans had the same bad habits of littering, unsanitary conditions, cluster, noise-making and indiscipline as experienced in many developing countries today.[24] The battle was certainly tough for the government. But it was persistence that brought victory in the end. Reorientation of citizens was carried out under the Ministry of Education. The government was determined to nurture citizens to be disciplined, considerate and courteous.

Another attitude that accounted for Singapore's success was the desire for excellence. There was no room for mediocrity. By the late 70s for instance, when the old problems of unemployment and lack of investments had been surmounted, the government sought to find a way to improve the quality of the new investments. Education and skill level of workers were other areas considered for quality improvement. Singapore Airlines, for instance, was made to understand that it was not enough to merely show the national flag but to strive to be competitive and self-supporting in order to survive and remain profitable.

The same success cannot be recorded for some developing countries simply because neither government nor citizens are prepared to change their attitude towards development. Both groups of stakeholders settle for mediocrity. Little progress can be expected as long as individuals continue to be self-centred and make little effort to work towards what would be profitable for everyone in society. What every society needs are a fair and firm leadership and a disciplined people.

Conclusion

Discussions in this chapter reveal that it is not enough for the government to be pragmatic. The people must have the same attitude in order for programmes to come to reality. At the same time, it is important that citizens undergo change management to help psych them to tread new paths. It was a united, trustworthy and determined group of leaders, backed by a practical, hardworking and trusting people that made success possible in Singapore. The next chapter is the concluding part of the research.

CHAPTER FOUR

CONCLUSIONS AND RECOMMENDATIONS FOR AFRICAN LEADERS

This chapter provides the summary of findings and conclusions as well as recommendations for African leaders.

There is evidence in the analysis so far pointing to the fact that the search for development paradigms by developing countries continues unabated. It is also evident that Western paradigms do not always offer the best solutions. Yet, indications are that, Western states will continue to interfere with the development process of developing countries as long as governments and people of the latter are not confident enough to face their unique challenges.

Again, it was realized that Singapore's development strategy was different from those of other Asian countries. This goes to buttress the point that each country is unique and must therefore seek unique measures.

Pragmatism helps to discover the uniqueness of each

country's situation. These arguments not withstanding, the reality is that no state is an island in the international system. Singapore has proven that it is no crime to borrow strategies from other countries as long as they contribute significantly to growth. Globalisation has made these facts even more pronounced. It is therefore important for countries to maintain friendly relations with neighbours to promote peace and facilitate knowledge sharing.

Another significant finding is that, apart from attitudinal change playing a primordial role, Singapore's government operated on three main principles to achieve and maintain progress. These include (a) Social cohesion through sharing the benefits of progress; (b) Equal opportunities for all; (c) Meritocracy (choosing the best man or woman for the job).

An important observation is that institutional reforms are facilitated by a stable economy and an efficient political system. In addition to this, a conducive business climate and high employee morale significantly boost productivity.

Findings also confirm the relevance of the theory of Economic Nationalism to the analysis. Discussions indicate that Africa, and for that matter developing countries, have not made significant progress mainly due to poor leadership. Singapore, on the other hand, had a strong leadership to wheel the state to prosperity. Furthermore, a country may be endowed with the necessary human and natural resources for growth, but without a committed government, these resources will be rendered "derelict." Drawing from the views of economic nationalists, it can be posited that it was a strong commitment to the national interest and the will to survive (amidst international pessimism) that motivated the government and people of Singapore to succeed.

CONCLUSIONS

This set out in the first chapter to test the hypothesis that a pragmatic approach to development will yield better results for Developing Countries than rigid paradigms.

The evidence adduced in this book leads to the conclusion that a pragmatic approach to development will yield better results for Developing Countries than rigid paradigms. This conviction is informed by Singapore's development experience, which reveals that, even though resource endowment and external factors may be unfavourable for a state, it takes pragmatic strategies to overcome limitations and reap success. Developing countries, on the other hand, have been on a buying spree for development paradigms for over forty years but results have not been too impressive. Additionally, Singapore's approach indicates that pragmatism finds expression in a government and people committed to the national interest, innovativeness as well as realistic and achievable policies.

The evidence from the study leads to the following

conclusions:

Land, capital and labour are not sufficient factors for national economic development. It is undeniable that political leadership plays a crucial role in moving a nation forward. This role can be likened to that of managing an individual firm, where management ensures that the most conducive environment is created for growth. Hence, the ability for the leadership to organise or mobilise all the productive units as well as the nature of laws and policies, determine the rate and manner in which national development takes place.

Another important determinant of efficiency and effectiveness of government operations is the kind of interactions and working relations that exist between political leaders and public servants. While public servants provide the expertise or technical knowledge, the government plays a critical role in the implementation process. The ability to implement policies hinges on the level of commitment to the cause in question.

The state of a nation's economy is highly dependent on the quality of relations existing between the government and citizens. Operating on a reciprocity principle, a citizen (or individual) is motivated to give to the state when it receives. Thus, where there is a right balance between the rights citizens enjoy and the duties expected of them by the state, the latter tends to enjoy a serene climate in which to operate.

The development process must therefore be a partnership rather than a one-sided initiative.

It is important that political leadership be charismatic enough to motivate the people to concentrate efforts in the right direction. This is because the people are the productive agents in the development process. The ability to harmonize individual and collective interests through appropriate policies is therefore crucial. To achieve this, governments will need to be knowledgeable of the interests of various groups.

Government alone cannot create development and jobs. When it attempts to do so it often leads to inefficiency and growing financial imbalances. The private sector must be included in the development plan. National objectives must be clearly spelt out to enable the private sector to make appropriate inputs. In this regard, private-public sector policies must be mutually supportive to achieve a holistic national development agenda. In addition to this it is important that policies/ projects are well coordinated among the various sectors.

While Singapore's historical circumstances at independence were similar to those felt by many Third World countries today, it will not be realistic to expect other nations to become as economically successful by simply replicating all elements of Singapore's strategy. What may work for one country may not necessarily work for another. What this research proposes is that governments and peoples of developing countries discover their uniqueness and work on finding pragmatic strategies that will yield positive results. The bottom line is to find out what is best for the country at any given point in time and how best decisions can be taken without putting the lives of future generations in jeopardy.

These conclusions confirm that the state remains the major actor in international relations. Governments cannot detach themselves from the role of state building. It is their highest responsibility not only to citizens but also to the international community as a whole.

RECOMMENDATIONS

Contrary to available evidence suggesting that Africa's future could be bleak, it is refreshing to note that the demand for change has become stronger than ever as realities indicate that Africa is perhaps worse off today than at independence. No longer are citizens content with simply being passive elements on which governments act. Citizens want to be an integral part of the development agenda. What African citizens are seeking are proactive governments who will bring about self-actualization.[1] This will be made possible through growth opportunities and equitable distribution of resources.

Informed by the above, this book makes a number of recommendations. It is important to note that in as much as the following recommendations target Africa, they are just as relevant to other developing countries outside Africa.

In agreement with Ndegwa, just like a person diagnosed with a serious disease hastens to find a cure (with more physical ability than normal), so must Africa react to her developmental challenges.[2]

The African condition calls for inventiveness and ingenuity in political leadership, in societal attitudes and in economic management. Africans must accept that solutions will not come from copying others per se, but by working towards unique solutions because the problems they face are unique.

African governments are advised to be selective in accepting advice from external experts. It must be borne in mind that no matter how good assistance appears, self-interest and power politics continue to underlie such advice. Foreign powers continue to be very keen to mould the continent and its people – all in a manner that serves their own purposes best.

What Africa needs now is a development-oriented leadership—not a political-liberation-focused leadership (whose mission is considered terminated). Governments must develop higher levels of managerial ability. This would ensure that a nation's management is ahead of evolving situations rather than being merely reduced to responding to crisis.

Africa will need to develop the capacity to manage development policies by (a) developing the ability to anticipate, plan for the future and outline routes required by defined objectives; (b) mobilise available potential resources; (c) guide, manage and monitor implementation of programmes; (d) continuously manage change through all the phases; (e) develop the skill of defining the respective roles of the major actors (government, private sector, civil society and external partners) to ensure proper coordination of the dynamics of the development process. This would ensure that each group of actors fulfils its role in a productive partnership.

Meanwhile constant supervision of managers in the government machinery (Ministries, Departments and Agencies) is critical for progress. This includes administering performance appraisals to assess progress.

African governments are advised to invest more into their intellectuals to enable the latter to study the continent and write more about it. This would ensure that proposed solutions are more in harmony with African conditions and aspirations. Incentives for African researchers may include the provision of effective intellectual property laws, high remuneration and awards in recognition of their invaluable contribution to development. Other incentives include a commitment by government to make available necessary logistics for research and to guarantee freedom of expression.

Another motivating strategy is for researches not to remain on library shelves, but to significantly influence policy-making.

An important step to self-sufficiency is for Africa to be able to meet the challenge of feeding her population in the future. In this regard, research efforts must be intensified and agricultural output at least doubled. Furthermore, Africa must develop efficient systems to manage the environment rather than leave the task to environmental experts (e.g. UN Environment Programme). A multidisciplinary and participatory approach must be adopted to involve the people in such efforts.

National unity must be promoted by breaking down barriers of tribalism. Citizens will need to undergo what could be termed development socialization to help educate them on the dynamics of the development process.

Given the high incidence of conflicts on the continent, it must be reiterated that, the key to peace and harmony in society is a sense of fairness, in which everyone has a share in the fruits of progress. Fairness can be achieved by ensuring equality before the law, irrespective of status, religion or ethnicity. Job opportunities must be based on meritocracy rather than nepotism. State revenue must find its way to the grassroots rather than be siphoned into individual pockets.

Although regionalism is being proposed as more or less the panacea to Africa's contemporary developmental challenges, little progress can be made unless transformation takes place in individual member countries. Transformation involves structural and institutional reforms. Reforms must aim at helping citizens rise above their basic needs to enable them pursue higher and more sophisticated goals. In other words, it is only when food, clothing and shelter are assured that individuals can be in a right frame of mind to strive for greater achievements. Transformation also involves investing more into education. There is no doubt that a highly educated populace will be in a better position to understand government policies and their implications on the future of the nation in question. Transformation will require a public service that sees its mission as that of serving the nation rather than as feeding on the nation. Nonetheless, the determining factor in achieving transformation is the commitment of governments. Governments must be prepared to graduate from mere signing of agreements/policies to actual effective and efficient *implementation.*

In all these efforts, attitudinal change and commitment by all stakeholders must be seen as the defining factor to set the tone for sustainable transformation. Attitudinal change would involve a complete shift from a dependency syndrome to that of a can-do-it approach. Attitudinal change also involves putting the national interest above individual interests.

APPENDIX I
SINGAPORE'S MOST SIGNIFICANT ACCOMPLISHMENTS OVER THE PAST 49 YEARS OF INDEPENDENCE

As many of you may be aware of, Singapore has been recognized as the best city for living in Asia, taking 26th place in this category globally. However, it's important to note that Singapore is among the most expensive cities in the world due to its high real estate prices and thriving business climate.

The country holds fifth position in the World Rating of Happiness, with Australia in first place, which in itself is one of the city-states greatest accomplishments. Singaporeans can owe this success to its strict laws and well-organized police service. Because of their exceptional social infrastructure, Singapore is rated the safest city in the world.

AN OUTLINE OF NOTABLE EVENTS IN SINGAPORE THAT HAVE LED TO SUCCESS

2002 January - Japan, Singapore sign free trade agreement.

Singapore's economic growth can be attributed partly to

the city-state's keenness to participate in free-trade agreements. Joining the Singapore-Japan free trade agreement boosted the economy in Singapore, and helped propel GDP per capita to over $60,000 before the 2007–2009 recession.

2005 - Singapore, Malaysia settle a bitter dispute over land reclamation work in border waters. Government approves a controversial plan to legalize casino gambling, paving way for construction of two multi-billion dollar casino resorts. President S. R. Nathan begins second term after winning elections from which his rivals were disqualified. Execution of an Australian man for drug smuggling, despite high-level appeals for clemency, is condemned by Australia's attorney-general as barbaric.

2007 January - Two African men are executed for drug smuggling despite worldwide appeals for clemency. Parliament votes against a proposal to decriminalize sex between men.

The decriminalization of same-sex laws in Singapore set a standard for equality and openness among their population, which is a large reason why the city-state continues to thrive today; lack of prejudice is essential for any city or country to prosper.

Headlines were made in January of 2007 when the Singapore law enforcement department decided to execute drug smugglers. The decision was highly controversial indeed, but sent a message to the world that Singapore was going to remain the world's safest city. Perhaps other countryies should follow their example!

October 2007: Singapore became the first to operate the world's biggest passenger plane, the Airbus A380 'superjumbo'.

• Singapore's role in global technological development is something to marvel at. Those in control of economic development in the city-state recognize that the air-travel industry is the future for global transportation, and being the fi st to produce the Airbus A380 (which remains one of the highest grossing commercial aircrafts o date) was a great move by Singapore to ensure future economic sustainability. On top of investing in the commercial plane industry, Singapore's Economic Development Board (EDB), the government agency tasked with attracting foreign companies to Singapore, says there is a big push underway toward innovation. "Innovation is a big theme," says EDB director of transport engineering division, Tan Kong Hwee, adding that it is important for aerospace companies – such as MRO companies – to innovate, so they can create value.

• To help with the push, the government announced on January 7, 2016 that it has budgeted SG$19 billion (US$13.2 billion) to be spent on science and technology research over five years starting in April 2016. Th s money is to be shared by all sectors of the economy, but Tan says a huge part of it will go into advanced manufacturing, which includes aerospace manufacturing.

2009 - Singapore appears to emerge from its worst recession on record after the economy expands at an annualized rate of 20.4% between April and June.

2012 January - Government-appointed committee recommends massive pay cuts for ministers including prime minister and president.

2012 May - Opposition Workers' Party wins closely fought by-election, retaining seat left e   pty after MP expelled by the party in February.

2014 March - Singapore becomes the second country in the world after the US to regulate virtual currencies such as bitcoins, in an attempt to prevent money-laundering.

Once bitcoin arrived, everyone suddenly got very excited, or indignant, or both. Life is too short to explain it in detail, but Wikipedia does a pretty good job. Suffice t to say that it's a virtual payment system that has no central repository and no single administrator, characteristics that have led the US Treasury to call it "a decentralized virtual currency". Because bitcoins can be transferred directly from one person to another, they are sometimes described as digital cash. And because the process by which bitcoins are "mined" involves computers carrying out complex cryptographically computations, it is often called a cryptocurrency.

Bitcoin divides the world into two camps: one (the majority) thinks that it must be some kind of scam; the other (comprised mostly of geeks and venture capitalists) thinks that it's the most interesting thing since, well, sliced bread. What excites the latter is bitcoin's formidable utility as a medium for online trading.

What is so enticing about Bitcoin you might ask? Well, because it is an online currency that is heavily regulated, the risk of theft nd fraud decrease considerably. The fact that Singapore has invested in online currencies is a testament to their sound economic forecasting.

2015 December - The United States says it is deploying specialized maritime surveillance plane to Singapore in an apparent response to China's pursuit of territorial claims in the South China Sea.

2016 May - Singapore says it will spend more than 1.5 billion dollars expanding the capacity of its military training bases in Australia as part of a 25-year agreement.

2016 August - Parliament approves a new contempt law which could see offenders jailed for up to three years. Human Rights Watch says the law could further impede freedom of speech and lead the media to self-censor.

The world's fi st driverless taxi service is launched in Singapore.

Singapore is without a doubt the most successful city-state on the planet. They have managed to sustain considerable economic growth since their independence; they have maintained very strict, yet effici   t law enforcement, while at the same time, assuring that their inhabitants are some of the happiest on the planet.

There are certainly a lot of lessons to be learned from Singapore; perhaps we will see more and more city-states emerging around the world due to their proficie t economic and social capabilities.

[Source: Retrieved on January 3, 2019 from | Singapore
profile - Timeline - BBC News Aviation Week | Wikipedia |
News, sport and opinion from the Guardian's US edition | The
Guardian]

APPENDIX II
CAN AFRICA SUSTAIN ITS RECENT STRONG ECONOMIC PERFORMANCES AND BENEFIT MORE FROM ITS ABUNDANT RESOURCES?

Since 2000 Africa's GDP has grown by 5.1% per year on average, nearly three times the rate of growth of the OECD area during the same period. In spite of recent country-specific challenges and headwinds from the global economy, growth is set to remain strong.

While the global crisis has affected Africa's growth performance, mainly because of weaker global demand, lower commodity prices and declines in capital flows, as well as promises of aid that never materialised, the outlook remains bright. Africa's economy is projected to grow by 4.8% in 2013 and 5.3 % in 2014, driven by increases in agricultural production, a buoyant services sector, and expansion in oil production and mining.

Africa's recent economic dynamism has been underpinned by sound macroeconomic policies and stronger partnerships with major emerging markets. The continent has become more resilient to shocks and has benefited from strong demand for commodities, increased investment flows and closer links to global value chains. Since 2000 Africa's exports have almost quadrupled in value, to close to US$582 billion in 2011. Better macroeconomic management has also helped, and the continent's average budget deficit is now close to zero.

STRUCTURAL CHALLENGES

Nearly 78% of the population of sub-Saharan Africa lives in poverty, with some 49% living below the international poverty line of \$1.25 per day in 2010. Africa will probably be the only developing region not to reach the Millennium Development Goal of halving poverty by 2015, and will struggle to reach the other goals as well. Only a third of Africans have access to sanitation, and another third have no access at all to clean water. Under such conditions fi hting diseases remains an uphill battle.

In addition, the predicament of Africa's fragile states, whose 200 million inhabitants need constant support, underlines the importance of development aid and the need for donors to reverse falling aid trends.

Education and job creation are also a priority. About 40 million young people are jobless, and youth unemployment reaches nearly 25% in Egypt and 50% in South Africa. The International Labour Organization (ILO) estimates that between 2000 and 2008 Africa created 73 million jobs, of which only 16 million were for 15 to 24 year olds.

Inequality is another serious concern, as wealth disparities in Africa are among the widest in the world. In 2010, 6 of the 10 most unequal countries in the world were in sub-Saharan Africa. Progress in reducing inequality has been slow, even as Africa's growth has picked up.

Another factor hindering progress is the gender gap, with sub-Saharan Africa registering the highest level of gender inequality. Th s affects productivity and growth. The UN Food and Agriculture Organization (FAO) estimates that if women farmers had the same access to productive resources as men, the resulting gains in agricultural productivity could lift s many as 150 million people out of hunger.

ACHIEVING STRUCTURAL TRANSFORMATION

Africa has to transform its economic structures so that its population can benefit from stronger, more inclu-sive growth. How can such a structural transformation be achieved?

The continent has a strong comparative advantage in natural resources, whether in energy, mineral resources or agriculture, which could be the basis for action. The OECD recommends a four-layered policy approach:

The first layer consists of adopting policies designed to improve infrastructure, logistics and skills, as well as promoting private sector development. For instance, in South Africa, if constraints such as infrastructure bottlenecks, water scarci-ty, and skills and energy shortages were resolved, the mining sector could potentially grow by 3% to 4% annually until 2020 and generate at least 300,000 jobs.

A second layer consists of strengthening the natural resource sector through greater investments in value added activities and know-how, thereby generating more revenue for government and more job opportunities for Africans.

The third layer involves managing natural resources more efficiently and sustainably, putting in place a transpar-ent and fair tax system, as well as promoting competition and fighting public and private corruption.

The fourth layer involves initiatives to raise agricultural productivity and build linkages to and from the extractive industries.

The time is ripe for Africa to make better use of its nat-ural resources and achieve more inclusive growth. The OECD is committed to working alongside African policymakers in this effort. We can share experiences and help design better policies through our dialogue and global forums. With the right policies and strategic approach, the social and economic progress of recent years could be the prelude to long-lasting, sustained prosperity in Africa.

[Sources: www.oecdobserver.org/angelgurria/www.oecd. org/about/secretary-general/www.oecd.org/africa/© OECD Observer No 296 Q3 2013]

ENDNOTES

INTRODUCTION

Black, J.K., <u>Development in Theory and Practice: Bridging the Gap.</u> (Boulder: Westview Press, Inc., 1991), p. 81.

Asante, S.K.B., <u>Building Capacity in African Regional Integration</u>. (Ghana Institute of Management and Public Administration, 2007), p. 29.

Gilpin R., <u>The Political Economy of International Relations</u>. (New Jersey: Princeton University Press, 1987), p.31.

Ibid., p. 32.

Mason, M., <u>Development and Disorder: A History of the Third World Since 1945</u>. (Hanover: University Press of New England, 1997), pp. 1-16.

Ibid., p. 5.

Ibid., p. 461.

Blomstrom M. et.al, <u>Development Theory in Transition. The Dependency Debate and Beyond: Third World Responses.</u> (London: Zed Books, 1984), pp. 6-7.

Ibid., p. 135.

Black, J.K., op.cit., pp. 1-17.

Ibid., p. 2.

Ibid., pp. 81-200.

Haggard, S., <u>Pathways from the Periphery: The Politics of Growth in the Newly Industrializing Countries</u> (New York: Cornell University Press, 1990), pp. 1-5.

Ibid., pp. 268-270.

Kuan Yew, L., <u>From Third World to First: The Singapore Story: 1965-2000</u> (New York: Harper Collins Publishers Inc., 2000), pp.1-9.

Ibid., pp. 685-691.

Onimode et.al., <u>African Development and Governance Strategies in the Twenty First Century: Looking Back to Move Forward</u> (London: Zed Books, 2004), pp. 1-30.

Ibid., pp. xv-xvi.

CHAPTER ONE

[1]   Kuan Yew, L., <u>From Third World to First: The Singapore Story: 1965 – 2000</u>. (New York: Harper Collins Publishers Inc., 2000), p.58.

[2] Microsoft Encarta Encyclopaedia 2005. © 1993-2004

Microsoft Corporation.

³ op.cit. p. 3.

Ibid., p. 7.

Ibid., pp.4-5.

Ibid., p. 6.

Ibid., pp. 7-8.

⁸ Ibid.

⁹ Cho-oon, K., "Singapore" in Marsh, I., Blondel, J., and Inoguchi T. (eds.) <u>Democracy, Governance, and Economic Performance: East and Southeast Asia</u>. (Tokyo: United Nations University Press, 1999), p. 289.

¹⁰ Ibid., p. 294.

Ibid., p. 289.

Kuan Yew, L. op.cit., p. 131.

Ibid., p. 200.

Ibid., pp. 158-159.

Arvis, J-F., Berenbeim, R.E., <u>Fighting Corruption in East Asia: Solutions from the Private Sector</u>. (Washington D.C.: World Bank, 2003), pp. 157-159.

¹⁶ Kuan Yew, L., op.cit., p.160.

[17] Ibid., pp. 212-214.

Waleed Haider, M., <u>Judiciary-Led Reforms in Singapore: Framework, Strategies, and Lessons</u>. (Washington D.C.: World Bank, 2007), pp. xv-xvi.

Ibid., p. xvii.

Ibid., p. xviii.

[21] Kuan Yew, L., op.cit., pp. 14-17.

Ibid., pp. 135-144.

[23] Cho-oon, K., op.cit., p. 290.

[24] Op.cit., p. 143.

Ibid. pp. 95-107.

[26] Cho-oon, K., op.cit., p. 298.

[27] Ibid., p. 300.

[28] Kuan Yew, L., op.cit., p. 63.

[29] Haggard, S., <u>Pathways from the Periphery: The Politics of Growth in the Newly Industrializing Countries</u>. (New York: Cornell University Press, 1990), pp. 111-112.

Op.cit., pp. 83-93.

[31] Ibid., p. 53.

[32] Ibid., pp. 54-55.

Lee. 173-184.

Cho-oon, K., op.cit., p. 302.

[35] Lai. D., 'Growth of Research and Development in Singapore 2000-2005', in <u>Statistics Singapore Newsletter</u>. March 2007, pp.1-7. http://www.singstat.gov.sg/pubn/papers/economy/ssnmar07-pg1-7.pdf . Assessed on 17th July 2008.

Meng Chung L., 'Infocomm Usage by Households and Individuals', in <u>Statistics Singapore Newsletter.</u> March 2006, p. 19. http://unpan1.un.org/intradoc/groups/public/documents/APCITY/UNPAN024566.pdf . Assessed on 17th July 2008.

CHAPTER TWO

Osaghae, E., "Introduction: Between the Individual and the State in Africa: The Imperative of Development" in Osaghae, E., (ed.) <u>Between State and Civil Society in Africa: Perspectives on Development</u>. (Senegal: CODESRIA Book Series, 1994), p. 4.

Ibid., p. 5.

ECOWAS, <u>Visions of a Better Tomorrow: NEPAD, ECOWAS, and AU</u>. (2001), pp. i-iii.

Antwi-Danso, V., "Regionalism and Economic Integration in Africa: Challenges and Prospects" in Legon Journal of International Affairs. Vol. 3 No. 2 November

2006, p. 152.

Osaghae, E., op.cit., p. 6.

Ibid., pp. 9-10.

Ibid., p. 11.

Ibid., pp. 11-12.

Onimode, B., "Mobilisation for the Implementation of Alternative Development Paradigms in the 21st-Century

Africa" in Onimode et al., <u>African Development and Governance Strategies in the Twenty First Century: Looking Back to Move Forward</u> (London: Zed Books, 2004), p. 21-23.

CHAPTER THREE

Research by Rastin, T., titled "Model for Development: A Case Study of Singapore's Economic Growth" in <u>Critique: A Worldwide Student Journal of Politics</u>. p.1. <u>http://lilt.ilstu.edu/critique/Fall%202003%20docs/TaymazFinal.pdf</u>. Accessed on 22nd July 2008

Rastin, T., op.cit. p. 1.

Ibid.

Ibid., p. 2.

Kuan Yew, L., <u>From Third World to First: The Singapore</u>

Story: 1965 – 2000. (New York: Harper Collins Publishers Inc., 2000), p. 8.

Ibid., p. 35.

Op.cit., 3.

Ibid.

Arvis, J-F., Berenbeim, R.E., Fighting Corruption in East Asia: Solutions from the Private Sector. (Washington D.C.: World Bank, 2003), pp. 157.

Rastin, T., op.cit. p. 6.

Ibid., p. 4.

Ibid., p. 6.

Kuan Yew, L., op.cit., p. 91.

Ibid., p. 93.

Ibid., p. 687.

Ibid., p. 99.

Ibid., p. 199.

Waleed Haider, M., Judiciary-Led Reforms in Singapore: Framework, Strategies, and Lessons. (Washington D.C.: World Bank, 2007) p. xxiii.

Cho-oon, K., "Singapore" in Marsh, I., Blondel, J., and Inoguchi T. (eds.) Democracy, Governance, and Economic Performance: East and Southeast Asia. (Tokyo: United

Nations University Press, 1999), pp. 296-297.

Kuan Yew, L., op.cit., p. 690.

Ibid., p. 20.

Ibid., p. 155.

Rastin, T., op.cit. p. 4.

Ibid., p. 174.

CHAPTER FOUR

Osaghae, E., "Introduction: Between the Individual and the State in Africa: The Imperative of Development" in Osaghae, E., (ed.) <u>Between State and Civil Society in Africa: Perspectives on Development</u>. (Senegal: CODESRIA Book Series, 1994), p. 2.

Ndegwa, P., <u>The African Challenge: In Search of Appropriate Development Strategies</u>. (Nairobi: Heinemann Kenya Limited, 1986). p. 4.

BIBLIOGRAPHY

A. BOOKS

Asante, S.K.B., Building Capacity in African Regional Integration. (Ghana Institute of Management and Public Administration, 2007).

Arvis, J-F., Berenbeim, R.E., Fighting Corruption in East Asia: Solutions from the Private Sector. (Washington D.C.: World Bank, 2003).

Black, J.K., Development in Theory and Practice: Bridging the Gap. (Boulder: Westview Press, Inc., 1991).

Blomstrom M. et.al, Development Theory in Transition. The Dependency Debate and Beyond: Third World Responses. (London: Zed Books, 1984).

Gilpin R., The Political Economy of International Relations. (New Jersey: Princeton University Press, 1987).

Haggard, S., Pathways from the Periphery: The Politics of Growth in the Newly Industrializing Countries (New York: Cornell University Press, 1990).

Kuan Yew, L., From Third World to First: The Singapore Story: 1965-2000 (New York: Harper Collins Publishers Inc.,

2000).

Mason, M., *Development and Disorder: A History of the Third World Since 1945*. (Hanover: University Press of New England, 1997).

Ndegwa, P., *The African Challenge: In Search of Appropriate Development Strategies*. (Nairobi: Heinemann Kenya Limited, 1986).

Waleed Haider, M., *Judiciary-Led Reforms in Singapore: Framework, Strategies, and Lessons*. (Washington D,C.: World Bank, 2007).

B. JOURNAL ARTICLES

Antwi Danso, V., "Regionalism and Economic Integration in Africa: Challenges and Prospects" in *Legon Journal of International Affairs*. Vol.3 No. 2 November 2006.

Cho-oon, K., "Singapore" in Marsh, I., Blondel, J., and Inoguchi T. (eds.) *Democracy, Governance, and Economic Performance: East and Southeast Asia*. (Tokyo: United Nations University Press, 1999).

ECOWAS, *Visions of a Better Tomorrow: NEPAD, ECOWAS, and AU*. (2001).

Kankwenda, M., "Forty Years of Development Illusions: Revisiting Development Policies and Practices in Africa" in Onimode et al., African Development and Governance Strategies in the Twenty First Century: Looking Back to Move Forward (London: Zed Books, 2004).

Onimode et.al., African Development and Governance Strategies in the Twenty First Century: Looking Back to Move Forward (London: Zed Books, 2004).

Onimode, B., "Mobilisation for the Implementaion of Alternative Development Paradigms in the 21st- Century Africa" in Onimode et al., African Development and Governance Strategies in the Twenty First Century: Looking Back to Move Forward (London: Zed Books, 2004).

Osaghae, E., "Introduction: Between the Individual and the State in Africa: The Imperative of Development" in Osaghae, E., (ed.) Between State and Civil Society in Africa: Perspectives on Development. (Senegal: CODESRIA Book Series, 1994).

C. WEBSITES

Lai. D., "Growth of Research and Development in Singapore 2000-2005", in Statistics Singapore Newsletter. March 2007.   http://www.singstat.gov.sg/pubn/

papers/economy/ssnmar07-pg1-7.pdf. Assessed on 17th July 2008.

Meng Chung L., 'Infocomm Usage by Households and Individuals', in Statistics Singapore Newsletter. March 2006. http://unpan1.un.org/intradoc/groups/public/documents/APCITY/UNPAN024566.pdf. Assessed on 17th July 2008.

Research by Rastin, T., titled "Model for Development: A case Study of Singapore's Economic Growth" in Critique: A Worldwide Student Journal of Politics. http://lilt.ilstu.edu/critique/Fall%202003%20docs/TaymazFinal.pdf. Accessed on 22nd July 2008.

Lecture delivered by Prof. Stiglitz on the topic: "Transforming African Economies: Lessons from Asia." http://myjoyonline.com/news/200807/18061.asp. Accessed on 9th July 2008.

Microsoft Encarta Encyclopedia 2005. © 1993-2004 Microsoft Corporation.